God:
Hit or Myth?

THE
RATIONALIST
PRESS

an imprint of

Wheaton Partners, Inc.

West Des Moines, Iowa

To order books direct from the publisher
www.ForBetterBooks.com

For additional information about
Wheaton Partners, Inc., its imprints
and trade distributor, please see
www.wheatonpartners.com

God:
Hit or Myth?

Robert Green Ingersoll

Ian Tarquin Hume, Editor

THE
RATIONALIST
PRESS

ISBN 0-9771489-0-4 (acid-free paper)

Published in the United States of America
Manufactured in the United States of America

First Edition

*For those who value the gifts of reason
and rational thought*
—Ian Tarquin Hume, Editor

God:
Hit or Myth?

1

For the most part we inherit our opinions. We are the heirs of habits and mental customs. Our beliefs, like the fashion of our garments, depend on where we were born. We are molded and fashioned by our surroundings.

Environment is a sculptor—a painter. If we had been born in Constantinople, the most of us would have said, "There is no God but Allah, and Mohammed is his prophet." If our parents had lived on the banks of the Ganges, we would have been worshipers of Shiva, longing for the heaven of Nirvana.

As a rule, children love their parents, believe what they teach, and take great pride in saying that the religion of mother is good enough for them. Most people love peace; they do not like to differ with their neighbors; they like company; they are social; they enjoy traveling on the highway with the multitude; they hate to walk alone.

The Scots are Calvinists because their fathers were. The Irish are Catholics because their fathers were. The English are Episcopalians because their fathers were. And the Americans are divided in a hundred sects because their fathers were. This is the general rule, to which there are many exceptions. Children sometimes are superior to their parents, modify their ideas, change their customs, and arrive at different conclusions. But this is generally so gradual that the departure is scarcely noticed, and those who change usually insist that they are still following the fathers.

It is claimed by Christian historians that the religion of a nation was sometimes suddenly changed, and that millions of Pagans were made into Christians by the command of a king. Philosophers do not agree with these historians. Names have been changed, altars have been overthrown, but opinions, customs and beliefs remained the same. A Pagan, beneath the drawn sword of a Christian, would probably change his religious views; and a Christian, with a scimitar above his head, might suddenly become a Mohammedan; but as a matter of fact both would remain exactly as they were before—except in speech.

Belief is not subject to the will. Men think as they must. Children do not, and cannot,

believe exactly as they were taught. They are
not exactly like their parents. They differ in
temperament, in experience, in capacity, in
surroundings. And so there is a continual,
though almost imperceptible, change. There
is development, conscious and unconscious
growth and, by comparing long periods of
time, we find that the old has been almost aban-
doned, almost lost in the new. Men cannot remain stationary. The mind cannot be securely
anchored. If we do not advance, we go back-
ward. If we do not grow, we decay. If we do not
develop, we shrink and shrivel.

Like the most of you, I was raised among
people who knew—who were certain. They did
not reason or investigate. They had no doubts.
They knew that they had the truth. In their
creed there was no guess—no perhaps. They
had a revelation from God. They knew the beginning of things. They knew that God com-
menced to create one Monday morning, four
thousand and four years before Christ. They
knew that in the eternity—back of that morning, he had done nothing. They knew that it
took him six days to make the Earth—all plants,
all animals, all life, and all the globes that wheel

in space. They knew exactly what he did each day and when he rested. They knew the origin, the cause of evil, of all crime, of all disease and death.

They not only knew the beginning, but they knew the end. They knew that life had one path and one road. They knew that the path—grass-grown and narrow, filled with thorns and net-tles, infested with vipers, wet with tears, stained by bleeding feet—led to heaven, and that the road—broad and smooth, bordered with fruits and flowers, filled with laughter and song and all the happiness of human love—led straight to hell. They knew that God was doing his best to make you take the path, and that the Devil used every art to keep you in the road.

They knew that there was a perpetual battle waged between the great powers of good and evil for the possession of human souls. They knew that many centuries ago God had left his throne and had been born a babe into this poor world; that he had suffered death for the sake of man, for the sake of saving a few. They also knew that the human heart was utterly de-praved, so that man by nature was in love with wrong and hated God with all his might.

At the same time they knew that God created man in his own image and was perfectly satisfied with his work. They also knew that he had been thwarted by the Devil, who with wiles and lies had deceived the first of humankind. They knew that in consequence of that, God cursed the man and woman; the man with toil, the woman with slavery and pain, and both with death; and that he cursed the Earth itself with briers and thorns, brambles and thistles. All these blessed things they knew. They knew, too, all that God had done to purify and elevate the race. They knew all about the Flood, knew that God—with the exception of eight—drowned all his children, the old and young, the bowed patriarch and the dimpled babe, the young man and the merry maiden, the loving mother and the laughing child, because his mercy endureth forever. They knew too, that he drowned the beasts and birds, everything that walked or crawled or flew, because his loving kindness is over all his works. They knew that God, for the purpose of civilizing his children, had devoured some with earthquakes, destroyed some with storms of fire, killed some with his lightning, millions with famine, with pestilence, and sacrificed countless thousands upon the fields of war. They knew that it was necessary to believe these things and to love God. They knew that there could be no salvation except by faith, and through the atoning blood of Jesus Christ.

All who doubted or denied would be lost. To live a moral and honest life, to keep your contracts, to take care of wife and child, to make a happy home, to be a good citizen, a patriot, a just and thoughtful man, was simply a respectable way of going to hell.

God did not reward men for being honest, generous and brave, but for the act of faith. Without faith, all the so-called virtues were sins and the men who practiced these virtues, without faith, deserved to suffer eternal pain.

All of these comforting and reasonable things were taught by the ministers in their pulpits, by teachers in Sunday schools, and by parents at home. The children were victims. They were assaulted in the cradle, in their mothers' arms. Then, the schoolmaster carried on the war against their natural sense, and all the books they read were filled with the same impossible truths. The poor children were helpless. The atmosphere they breathed was filled with lies, lies that mingled with their blood.

In those days ministers depended on revivals to save souls and reform the world. In the winter, navigation having closed, business was mostly suspended. There were no railways and the only means of communication were wagons and boats. Generally the roads were so bad that the wagons were laid up with the boats. There were no operas, no theaters, no amusement except parties and balls. The parties were regarded as worldly and the balls as wicked. For real and virtuous enjoyment the good people depended on revivals.

The sermons were mostly about the pains and agonies of hell, the joys and ecstasies of heaven, salvation by faith, and the efficacy of the atonement. The little churches in which the services were held were generally small, badly ventilated, and exceedingly warm. The emotional sermons, the sad singing, the hysterical amens, the hope of heaven, the fear of hell, caused many to lose the little sense they had. They became substantially insane. In this condition they flocked to the 'mourner's bench,' asked for the prayers of the faithful, had strange feelings, prayed and wept, and thought they had been 'born again.' Then they would tell their experience, how wicked they had been, how evil had been their thoughts, their desires, and how good they had suddenly become.

They used to tell the story of an old woman who, in telling her experience, said:

> *Before I was converted, before I gave my heart to God, I used to lie and steal, but now, thanks to the grace and blood of Jesus Christ, I have quit 'em both, in a great measure.*

Of course all the people were not exactly of one mind. There were some scoffers, and now and then some man had sense enough to laugh at the threats of priests and make a jest of hell. Some would tell of unbelievers who had lived and died in peace.

When I was a boy I heard them tell of an old farmer in Vermont. He was dying. The minister was at his bed-side and asked him if he was a Christian, if he was prepared to die. The old man answered that he had made no preparation, that he was not a Christian, that he had never done anything but work. The preacher said that he could give him no hope unless he had faith in Christ, and that if he had no faith his soul would certainly be lost. The old man was not frightened. He was perfectly calm. In a weak and broken voice he said:

> *Mr. Preacher, I suppose you noticed my farm. My wife and I came here more than fifty years ago. We were just married. It was a forest then and the land was covered with stones. I cut down the trees, burned the logs, picked up the stones and laid the walls. My wife spun and wove and worked every moment. We raised and educated our children—denied ourselves. During all these years my wife never had a good dress, or a decent bonnet. I never had a good suit of clothes. We lived on the plainest food. Our hands, our bodies are deformed by toil. We never had a vacation. We loved each other and the children. That is the only luxury we ever had. Now I am about to die and you ask me if I am prepared. Mr. Preacher, I have no fear of the future, no terror of any other world. There may be such a place as hell—but if*

there is, you never can make me believe that it's any worse than old Vermont.

So, they told of a man who compared himself with his dog. "My dog," he said, "just barks and plays—has all he wants to eat. He never works, has no trouble about business. In a little while he dies, and that is all. I work with all my strength. I have no time to play. I have trouble every day. In a little while I will die, and then I go to hell. I wish that I had been a dog."

Well, while the cold weather lasted, while the snows fell, the revival went on, but when the winter was over, when the steamboat's whistle was heard, when business started again, most of the converts 'backslid' and fell again into their old ways. But the next winter they were on hand, ready to be 'born again.' They formed a kind of stock company, playing the same parts every winter and backsliding every spring.

The ministers, who preached at these revivals, were in earnest. They were zealous and sincere. They were not philosophers. To them science was the name of a vague dread, a dangerous enemy. They did not know much, but they believed a great deal. To them hell was a burning reality. They could see the smoke and flames. The Devil was no myth. He was an actual person, a rival of God, an enemy of mankind. They thought that the important business of this life was to save your soul; that all should resist and scorn the pleasures of sense, and keep their eyes steadily fixed on the golden gate of the New Jerusalem. They were unbalanced, emotional, hysterical, bigoted, hateful, loving, and insane. They really believed the Bible to be the actual word of God, a book without mistake or contradiction. They called its cruelties, justice; its absurdities, mysteries; its miracles, facts; and the idiotic passages were regarded as profoundly spiritual. They dwelt on the pangs, the regrets, the infinite agonies of the lost, and showed how easily they could be avoided and how cheaply heaven could be obtained. They told their hearers to believe, to have faith, to give their hearts to God, their sins to Christ, who would bear their burdens and make their souls as white as snow. All this the ministers really believed. They were absolutely certain. In their minds the Devil had tried in vain to sow the seeds of doubt.

I heard hundreds of these evangelical sermons; heard hundreds of the most fearful and vivid descriptions of the tortures inflicted in hell, of the horrible state of the lost. I supposed that what I heard was true and yet I did not believe it. I said, "It is," and then I thought: 'It cannot be.' These sermons made but faint impressions on my mind. I was not convinced. I had no desire to be 'converted,' did not want a 'new heart' and had no wish to be 'born again.'

But I heard one sermon that touched my heart, one that left its mark, like a scar, on my brain. One Sunday I went with my brother to hear a Free Will Baptist preacher. He was a large man, dressed like a farmer, but he was an orator. He could paint a picture with words. He took for his text the parable of the rich man and Lazarus. He described Dives, the rich man: his manner of life; the excesses in which he indulged; his extravagance; his riotous nights; his purple and fine linen; his feasts; his wines; and his beautiful women. Then he described Lazarus: his poverty; his rags and wretchedness; his poor body eaten by disease; the crusts and crumbs he devoured; the dogs that pitied him. He pictured his lonely life, his friendless death.

Then, changing his tone of pity to one of triumph, leaping from tears to the heights of exultation, from defeat to victory, he described the glorious company of angels, who with white and outspread wings carried the soul of the despised pauper to Paradise, to the bosom of Abraham.

Then, changing his voice to one of scorn and loathing, he told of the rich man's death. He was in his palace, on his costly couch, the air heavy with perfume, the room filled with servants and physicians. His gold was worthless then. He could not buy another breath. He died, and in hell he lifted up his eyes, being in torment.

Then, assuming a dramatic attitude, putting his right hand to his ear, he whispered:

> *Hark! I hear the rich man's voice. What does he say? Hark! Father Abraham! Father Abraham! I pray thee send Lazarus that he may dip the tip of his finger in water and cool my parched tongue, for I am tormented in this flame.*

"Oh, my hearers, he has been making that request for more than eighteen hundred years. And millions of ages hence that wail will cross the gulf that lies between the saved and lost and still will be heard the cry: 'Father Abraham! Father Abraham! I pray thee send Lazarus that he may dip the tip of his finger. in water and cool my parched tongue, for I am tormented in this flame.'"

For the first time I understood the dogma of eternal pain, appreciated "the glad tidings of great Joy." For the first time my imagination grasped the height and depth of the Christian horror. Then I said, "It is a lie, and I hate your religion. If it is true, I hate your God."

From that day I have had no fear, no doubt. For me, on that day, the flames of hell were quenched. From that day I have passionately hated every orthodox creed. That sermon did some good.

II

From my childhood I had heard read, and read the Bible myself. Morning and evening the sacred volume was opened and prayers were said. The Bible was my first history, the Jews were the first people, and the events narrated by Moses and the other inspired writers, and those predicted by prophets were the all-important things. In other books were found the thoughts and dreams of men, but in the Bible were the sacred truths of God.

Yet in spite of my surroundings, of my education, I had no love for God. He was so saving of mercy, so extravagant in murder, so anxious to kill, so ready to assassinate, that I hated him with all my heart. At his command, babes were butchered, women violated, and the white hair of trembling age stained with blood. This God visited the people with pestilence; filled the houses and covered the streets with the dying and the dead; saw babes starving on the empty breasts of pallid mothers; heard the sobs, saw the tears, the sunken cheeks, the sightless eyes, the new made graves; and remained as pitiless as the pestilence.

This God withheld the rain, caused the famine; saw the fierce eyes of hunger, the wasted forms, the white lips; saw mothers eating babes; and remained ferocious as famine. It seems to me impossible for a civilized man to love or worship, or respect the God of the Old Testament. A really civilized man, a really civilized woman, must hold such a God in abhorrence and contempt.

But in the old days the good people justified Jehovah in his treatment of the heathen. The wretches who were murdered were idolaters and therefore unfit to live. According to the Bible, God had never revealed himself to these people and he knew that without a revelation they could not know that he was the true God. Whose fault was it then that they were heathen? The Christians said that God had the right to destroy them because he created them. What did he create them for? He knew when he made them that they would be food for the sword. He knew that he would have the pleasure of seeing them murdered.

As a last answer, as a final excuse, the worshipers of Jehovah said that all these horrible things happened under the 'old dispensation' of unyielding law and absolute justice, but that now under the 'new dispensation,' all had been changed—the sword of justice had been sheathed and love enthroned. In the Old Testament, they said God is the judge, but in the New, Christ is the merciful. As a matter of fact, the New Testament is infinitely worse than the Old. In the Old there is no threat of eternal pain. Jehovah had no eternal prison, no everlasting fire. His hatred ended at the grave. His revenge was satisfied when his enemy was dead. In the New Testament, death is not the end, but the beginning of punishment that has no end. In the New Testament the malice of God is infinite and the hunger of his revenge eternal.

The orthodox God, when clothed in human flesh, told his disciples not to resist evil, to love their enemies, and when smitten on one cheek to turn the other. And yet, we are told that this same God, with the same loving lips, uttered these heartless, these fiendish words: "Depart ye cursed into everlasting fire, prepared for the Devil and his angels." These are the words of 'eternal love.' No human being has imagination enough to conceive of this infinite horror. All that the human race has suffered in war and want, in pestilence and famine, in fire and flood; all the pangs and pains of every disease and every death; all this is as nothing compared with the agonies to be endured by one lost soul. This is the consolation of the Christian religion. This is the justice of God, the mercy of Christ.

This frightful dogma, this infinite lie, made me the implacable enemy of Christianity. The truth is that this belief in eternal pain has been the real persecutor. It founded the Inquisition, forged the chains, and furnished the fagots. It has darkened the lives of many millions. It made the cradle as terrible as the coffin. It enslaved nations and shed the blood of countless thousands. It sacrificed the wisest, the bravest and the best. It subverted the idea of justice, drove mercy from the heart, changed men to fiends and banished reason from the brain. Like a venomous serpent it crawls and coils and hisses in every orthodox creed. It makes man an eternal victim and God an eternal fiend. It is the one infinite horror. Every church in which it is taught is a public curse. Every preacher who teaches it is an enemy of mankind. Below this

Christian dogma savagery cannot go. It is the infinite of malice, hatred, and revenge. Nothing could add to the horror of hell, except the presence of its creator, God.

While I have life, as long as I draw breath, I shall deny with all my strength, and hate with every drop of my blood, this infinite lie. Nothing gives me greater joy than to know that this belief in eternal pain is growing weaker every day; that thousands of ministers are ashamed of it. It gives me joy to know that Christians are becoming merciful, so merciful that the fires of hell are burning low, flickering, choked with ashes, destined in a few years to die out forever.

For centuries Christendom was a madhouse. Popes, cardinals, bishops, priests, monks and heretics were all insane. Only a few—four or five in a century—were sound in heart and brain. Only a few, in spite of the roar and din, in spite of the savage cries, heard reason's voice. Only a few in the wild rage of ignorance, fear and zeal preserved the perfect calm that wisdom gives.

We have advanced. In a few years the Christians will become—let us hope—humane and sensible enough to deny the dogma that fills the endless years with pain. They ought to know

now that this dogma is utterly inconsistent with the wisdom, the justice, the goodness of their God. They ought to know that their belief in hell gives to the Holy Ghost—the Dove—the beak of a vulture, and fills the mouth of the Lamb of God with the fangs of a viper.

III

In my youth I read religious books: books about God, about the atonement, about salvation by faith, and about the other worlds. I became familiar with the commentators: with Adam Clark, who thought that the serpent seduced our mother Eve, and was in fact the father of Cain. He also believed that the animals, while in the ark, had their natures changed to that degree that they devoured straw together and enjoyed each other's society, thus prefiguring the blessed millennium.

I read Scott, who was such a natural theologian that he really thought the story of Phaeton, of the wild steeds dashing across the sky, corroborated the story of Joshua having stopped the sun and moon. So, I read Henry MacKnight and found that God so loved the world that he made up his mind to damn a large majority of the human race.

I read Cruden, who made the great Concordance, and made the miracles as small and probable as he could. I remember that he explained the miracle of feeding the wandering Jews with quails, by saying that even at this day immense numbers of quails crossed the Red Sea, and that sometimes when tired, they settled on ships that sank beneath their weight. The fact that the explanation was as hard to believe as the miracle made no difference to the devout Cruden.

To while away the time I read Calvin's Institutes, a book calculated to produce, in any natural mind, considerable respect for the Devil.

I read Paley's Evidences and found that the evidence of ingenuity in producing the evil, in contriving the hurtful, was at least equal to the evidence tending to show the use of intelligence in the creation of what we call good. You know the watch argument was Paley's greatest effort. A man finds a watch and it is so wonderful that he concludes that it must have had a maker. He finds the maker and he is so much more wonderful than the watch that he says he must have had a maker. Then he finds God, the maker of the man, and he is so much more wonderful than the man that he could not have had a maker. This is what the lawyers call a departure in pleading. According to Paley, there can be no design without a designer, but there can be a designer without a design. The wonder of the watch suggested the watchmaker, and the wonder of the watchmaker suggested the creator, and the wonder of the creator demonstrated that he was not created, but was uncaused and eternal.

We had Edwards on the will, in which the reverend author shows that necessity has no effect on accountability, and that when God creates a human being and at the same time determines and decrees exactly what that being shall do and be, the human being is responsible, and God in his justice and mercy has the right to torture the soul of that human being forever. Yet Edwards said that he loved God.

The fact is that if you believe in an infinite God, and also in eternal punishment, then you must admit that Edwards and Calvin were absolutely right. There is no escape from their conclusions if you admit their premises. They were infinitely cruel, their premises infinitely absurd, their God infinitely fiendish, and their logic perfect. And yet I have kindness and candor enough to say that Calvin and Edwards were both insane.

We had plenty of theological literature. There was Jenkyn on the atonement, who demonstrated the wisdom of God in devising a way in which the sufferings of innocence could justify the guilty. He tried to show that children could justly be punished for the sins of their ancestors, and that men could, if they had faith, be justly credited with the virtues of others. Nothing could be more devout, orthodox, and idiotic. But all of our theology was not in prose.

We had Milton with his celestial militia, with his great and blundering God, his proud and cunning Devil, his wars between immortals, and all the sublime absurdities that religion wrought within the blind man's brain. The theology taught by Milton was dear to the Puritan heart. It was accepted by New England and it poisoned the souls and ruined the lives of thousands. The genius of Shakespeare could not make the theology of Milton poetic. In the literature of the world there is nothing, outside of the 'sacred books,' more perfectly absurd.

We had Young's *Night Thoughts*, and I supposed that the author was an exceedingly devout and loving follower of the Lord. Yet, Young had a great desire to be a bishop and to accomplish that end he electioneered with the king's mistress. In other words, he was a fine old hypocrite. In the *Night Thoughts* there is scarcely a genuinely honest, natural line. It is pretence from beginning to end. He did not write what he felt, but what he thought he ought to feel.

We had Pollok's "Course of Time," with its worm that never dies, its quenchless flames, its endless pangs, its leering devils, and its gloating God. This frightful poem should have been written in a madhouse. In it you find all the cries and groans and shrieks of maniacs, when they tear and rend each other's flesh. It is as heartless, as hideous, and as hellish as the thirty-second chapter of Deuteronomy.

We all know the beautiful hymn commencing with the cheerful line: "Hark from the tombs, a doleful sound." Nothing could have been more appropriate for children. It is well to put a coffin where it can be seen from the cradle. When a mother nurses her child, an open grave should be at her feet. This would tend to make the babe serious, reflective, religious and miserable.

God hates laughter and despises mirth. To feel free, untrammeled, irresponsible, joyous; to forget care and death; to be flooded with sunshine without a fear of night; to forget the past; to have no thought of the future, no dream of God, or heaven, or hell; to be intoxicated with the present; to be conscious only of the clasp and kiss of the one you love; this is the sin against the Holy Ghost.

But we had Cowper's poems. Cowper was sincere. He was the opposite of Young. He had an observing eye, a gentle heart and a sense of the artistic. He sympathized with all who suffered; with the imprisoned, the enslaved and the outcasts. He loved the beautiful. No wonder that the belief in eternal punishment made this loving soul insane. No wonder that the 'tidings of great Joy' quenched Hope's great star and left his broken heart in the darkness of despair.

We had many volumes of orthodox sermons, filled with wrath and the terrors of the judgment to come—sermons that had been delivered by savage saints. We had *The Book of Martyrs*, showing that Christians had for many centuries imitated the God they worshiped. We had the history of the Waldenses, of the reformation of the Church. We had *Pilgrim's Progress*,

Baxter's Call and *Butler's Analogy*. To use a Western phrase or saying, I found that Bishop Butler dug up more snakes than he killed; suggested more difficulties than he explained, more doubts than he dispelled.

IV

Among such books my youth was passed. All the seeds of Christianity, of superstition, were sown in my mind and cultivated with great diligence and care. All that time I knew nothing of any science, nothing about the other side, nothing of the objections that had been urged against the blessed Scriptures, or against the perfect Congregational creed. Of course I had heard the ministers speak of blasphemers, of infidel wretches, of scoffers who laughed at holy things. They did not answer their arguments, but they tore their characters into shreds and demonstrated by the fury of assertion that they had done the Devil's work. And yet in spite of all I heard, of all I read, I could not quite believe. My brain and heart said, 'No.'

For a time I left the dreams, the insanities, the illusions and delusions, the nightmares of theology. I studied astronomy—just a little. I examined maps of the heavens, learned the names of some of the constellations, of some of the stars; found something of their size and the velocity with which they wheeled in their orbits; obtained a faint conception of astronomical spaces; found that some of the known stars were so far away in the depths of space that their light, traveling at the rate of nearly two hundred thousand miles a second, required many years to reach this little world; found that, compared with the great stars, our Earth was but a grain of sand—an atom; found that the old belief that all the hosts of heaven had been created for the benefit of man, was infinitely absurd.

I compared what was really known about the stars with the account of creation as told in Genesis. I found that the writer of the inspired book had no knowledge of astronomy; that he was as ignorant as a Choctaw chief, as an Eskimo driver of dogs. Does anyone imagine that the author of Genesis knew anything about the sun—its size; that he was acquainted with Sirius, the North Star, with Capella, or that he knew anything of the clusters of stars so far away that their light, now visiting our eyes, has been traveling for two million years? If he had known these facts would he have said that Jehovah worked nearly six days to make this world, and only a part of the afternoon of the fourth day to make the sun and moon and all the stars? Yet, millions of people insist that the writer of Genesis was inspired by the Creator of all worlds.

Now, intelligent men, who are not frightened, whose brains have not been paralyzed by fear, know that the sacred story of creation was written by an ignorant savage. The story is inconsistent with all known facts, and every star shining in the heavens testifies that its author was an uninspired barbarian.

I admit that this unknown writer was sincere, that he wrote what he believed to be true, that he did the best he could. He did not claim to be inspired, did not pretend that the story had been told to him by Jehovah. He simply stated the 'facts' as he understood them.

After I had learned a little about the stars I concluded that this writer, this 'inspired' scribe, had been misled by myth and legend, and that he knew no more about creation than the average theologian of my day. In other words, that he knew absolutely nothing.

And here, allow me to say that the ministers who are answering me are turning their guns in the wrong direction. These reverend gentlemen should attack the astronomers. They should malign and vilify Kepler, Copernicus, Newton, Herschel and Laplace. These men were the real destroyers of the sacred story. Then, after having disposed of them, they can wage a war against the stars and against Jehovah himself for having furnished evidence against the truthfulness of his book.

Then I studied geology—not much, just a little; just enough to find in a general way the principal facts that had been discovered, and some of the conclusions that had been reached. I learned something of the action of fire, of water, of the formation of islands and continents, of the sedimentary and igneous rocks, of the coal measures, of the chalk cliffs, something about coral reefs, about the deposits made by rivers, the effect of volcanoes, of glaciers, and of the all-surrounding sea; just enough to know that the Laurentian rocks were millions of years older than the grass beneath my feet; just enough to feel certain that this world had been pursuing its flight about the sun, wheeling in light and shade, for hundreds of millions of years; just enough to know that the 'inspired' writer knew nothing of the history of the Earth, nothing of the great forces of Nature, of wind and wave and fire; forces that have destroyed and built, wrecked and wrought through all the countless years.

And let me tell the ministers again that they should not waste their time in answering me. They should attack the geologists. They should deny the facts that have been discovered. They should launch their curses at the blaspheming seas, and dash their heads against the infidel rocks.

Then I studied biology—not much; just enough to know something of animal forms, enough to know that life existed when the Laurentian rocks were made; just enough to know that implements of stone, implements that had been formed by human hands, had been found mingled with the bones of extinct animals, bones that had been split with these implements, and that these animals had ceased to exist hundreds of thousands of years before the manufacture of Adam and Eve.

Then I felt sure that the 'inspired' record was false; that many millions of people had been deceived and that all I had been taught about the origin of worlds and men was utterly untrue. I felt that I knew that the Old Testament was the work of ignorant men; that it was a mingling of truth and mistake, of wisdom and foolishness, of cruelty and kindness, of philosophy and absurdity; that it contained some elevated thoughts, some poetry, a good deal of the solemn and commonplace; some hysterical, some tender, some wicked prayers, some insane predictions, some delusions, and some chaotic dreams.

Of course the theologians fought the facts found by the geologists, the scientists, and sought to sustain the sacred Scriptures. They mistook the bones of the mastodon for those of human beings, and by them proudly proved that, "there were giants in those days." They accounted for the fossils by saying that God had made them to try our faith, or that the Devil had imitated the works of the Creator.

They answered the geologists by saying that the 'days' in Genesis were long periods of time, and that, after all, the flood might have been local. They told the astronomers that the sun and moon were not actually, but only apparently, stopped. And that the appearance was produced by the reflection and refraction of light. They excused the slavery and polygamy, the robbery and murder upheld in the Old Testament by saying that the people were so degraded that Jehovah was compelled to pander to their ignorance and prejudice. In every way the clergy sought to evade the facts, to dodge the truth, to preserve the creed.

At first they flatly denied the facts. Then they belittled them. Then they harmonized them. Then they denied that they had denied them. Then they changed the meaning of the 'inspired' book to fit the facts. At first they said that if the facts, as claimed, were true, the Bible was false and Christianity itself a superstition. Afterward they said the facts, as claimed, were true and that they established beyond all doubt the inspiration of the Bible and the divine origin of orthodox religion. Anything they could not dodge, they swallowed; and anything they could not swallow, they dodged.

I gave up the Old Testament on account of its mistakes, its absurdities, its ignorance and its cruelty. I gave up the New because it vouched for the truth of the Old. I gave it up on account of its miracles, its contradictions, because Christ and his disciples believe in the existence of devils, talked and made bargains with them, expelled them from people and animals. This, of itself, is enough. We know—if we know anything—that devils do not exist; that Christ never cast them out; and that if he pretended to, he was either ignorant or dishonest or insane. These stories about devils demonstrate the human, the ignorant origin of the New Testament. I gave up the New Testament because it rewards credulity, and curses brave and honest men, and because it teaches the infinite horror of eternal pain.

V

Having spent my youth in reading books about religion, about the 'new birth,' the disobedience of our first parents, the atonement, salvation by faith, the wickedness of pleasure, the degrading consequences of love, and the impossibility of getting to heaven by being honest and generous, and having become somewhat weary of the frayed and raveled thoughts, you can imagine my surprise, my delight when I read the poems of Robert Burns.

I was familiar with the writings of the devout and insincere, the pious and petrified, the pure and heartless. Here was a natural honest man. I knew the works of those who regarded all Nature as depraved and looked upon love as the legacy and perpetual witness of original sin. Here was a man who plucked joy from the mire, made goddesses of peasant girls, and enthroned the honest man. One whose sympathy, with loving arms, embraced all forms of suffering life, who hated slavery of every kind, who was as natural as heaven's blue, with humor kindly as an autumn day, with wit as sharp as Ithuriel's spear, and scorn that blasted like the simoom's breath; a man who loved this world, this life, the things of every day, and placed above all else the thrilling ecstasies of human love.

I read and read again with rapture, tears and smiles, feeling that a great heart was throbbing in the lines. The religious, the lugubrious, the artificial, the spiritual poets were forgotten or remained only as the fragments, the half remembered horrors of monstrous and distorted dreams. I had found at last a natural man: one who despised his country's cruel creed, and was brave and sensible enough to say, "All religions are auld wives' fables, but an honest man has nothing to fear, either in this world or the world to come;" one who had the genius to write "Holy Willie's Prayer," a poem that crucified Calvinism and through its bloodless heart thrust the spear of common sense, a poem that made every orthodox creed the food of scorn, of inextinguishable laughter.

Burns had his faults, his frailties. He was intensely human. Still, I would rather appear at the 'Judgment Seat' drunk, and be able to say

that I was the author of "A man's a man for 'a
that," than to be perfectly sober and admit that
I had lived and died a Scot Presbyterian.

I read Byron; read his Cain, in which, as in
Paradise Lost, the Devil seems to be the better
god; read his beautiful, sublime and bitter lines;
read his "Prisoner of Chillon"—his best—a
poem that filled my heart with tenderness, with
pity, and with an eternal hatred of tyranny.

I read Shelley's "Queen Mab," a poem filled
with beauty, courage, thought, sympathy, tears
and scorn, in which a brave soul tears down the
prison walls and floods the cells with light. I
read his "Skylark," a winged flame, passionate
as blood, tender as tears, pure as light.

I read Keats, "whose name was writ in water;" read "St. Agnes Eve," a story told with such
an artless art that this poor common world is
changed to fairyland; the Grecian Urn, that
fills the soul with ever eager love, with all the
rapture of imagined song; "The Nightingale," a
melody in which there is the memory of morn,
a melody that dies away in dusk and tears, pain-
ing the senses with its perfectness.

And then I read Shakespeare, the plays, the
sonnets, the poems—read all. I beheld a new

heaven and a new Earth; Shakespeare, who knew the brain and heart of man, the hopes and fears, the loves and hatreds, the vices and the virtues of the human race; whose imagination read the tear-blurred records, the blood-stained pages of all the past, and saw—falling athwart the outspread scroll—the light of hope and love; Shakespeare, who sounded every depth while, on the loftiest peak, there fell the shadow of his wings. I compared the Plays with the 'inspired' books; "Romeo and Juliet" with the "Song of Solomon," Lear with Job, and the Sonnets with the Psalms, and I found that Jehovah did not understand the art of speech. I compared Shakespeare's women—his perfect women—with the women of the Bible. I found that Jehovah was not a sculptor, not a painter, not an artist; that he lacked the power that changes clay to flesh, the art, the plastic touch that molds the perfect form, the breath that gives it free and joyous life, the genius that creates the faultless. The sacred books of all the world are worthless dross and common stones compared with Shakespeare's glittering gold and gleaming gems.

VI

Up to this time I had read nothing against our blessed religion except what I had found in Burns, Byron and Shelley. By some accident I read Volney, who shows that all religions are, and have been, established in the same way; that all had their Christs, their apostles, miracles and sacred books; and then asked how it is possible to decide which is the true one. A question that is still waiting for an answer.

I read Gibbon, the greatest of historians, who marshaled his facts as skillfully as Caesar did his legions, and I learned that Christianity is only a name for Paganism—for the old religion—shorn of its beauty; that some absurdities had been exchanged for others; that some gods had been killed, a vast multitude of devils created, and that hell had been enlarged.

And then I read *The Age of Reason*, by Thomas Paine. Let me tell you something about this sublime and slandered man. He came to this country just before the Revolution. He brought a letter of introduction from Benjamin Franklin, at that time the greatest American. In Philadelphia, Paine was employed to write for the Pennsylvania Magazine. We know that he wrote at least five articles. The first was against slavery; the second against dueling; the third on the treatment of prisoners, showing that the object should be to reform, not to punish and degrade; the fourth on the rights of woman; and the fifth in favor of forming societies for the prevention of cruelty to children and animals. From this you see that he suggested the great reforms of our century.

The truth is that he labored all his life for the good of his fellow-men, and did as much to found the Great Republic as any man who ever stood beneath our flag. He gave his thoughts about religion, about the blessed Scriptures, about the superstitions of his time. He was perfectly sincere and what he said was kind and fair. *The Age of Reason* filled with hatred the hearts of those who loved their enemies, and the occupant of every orthodox pulpit became, and still is, a passionate maligner of Thomas Paine. No one has answered—no one will answer—his argument against the dogma of inspiration, his objections to the Bible. He did not rise above all the superstitions of his day. While he hated Jehovah, he praised the God of Nature, the creator and preserver of all. In this he was wrong, because, as Watson said in his "Reply to Paine," the God of Nature is as heartless, as cruel as the God of the Bible. But Paine was one of the pioneers, one of the Titans, one of the heroes, who gladly gave his life, his every thought and act, to free and civilize mankind.

I read Voltaire. Voltaire, the greatest man of his century, and who did more for liberty of thought and speech than any other being, human or 'divine.' Voltaire, who tore the mask from hypocrisy and found behind the painted smile the fangs of hate. Voltaire, who attacked the savagery of the law, the cruel decisions of venal courts, and rescued victims from the wheel and rack. Voltaire, who waged war against the tyranny of thrones, the greed and heartlessness of power. Voltaire, who filled the flesh of priests with the barbed and poisoned arrows of his wit and made the pious jugglers—who cursed him in public—laugh at themselves in private. Voltaire, who sided with the oppressed, rescued the unfortunate, championed the obscure and weak, civilized judges, repealed laws and abolished torture in his native land. In every direction this tireless man fought the absurd, the miraculous, the supernatural, the idiotic, and the unjust. He had no reverence for the ancient. He was not awed by pageantry and pomp, by crowned Crime or mitered Pretence. Beneath the crown he saw the criminal; under the miter, the hypocrite.

To the bar of his conscience, his reason, he summoned the barbarism and the barbarians of his time. He pronounced judgment against them all, and that judgment has been affirmed by the intelligent world. Voltaire lighted a torch and gave to others the sacred flame. The light still shines and will as long as man loves liberty and seeks for truth.

I read Zeno, the man who said, centuries before our Christ was born, that man could not own his fellow-man:

> *No matter whether you claim a slave by purchase or capture the title is bad. They, who claim to own their fellow-men, look down into the pit and forget the justice that should rule the world.*

I became acquainted with Epicurus, who taught the religion of usefulness, of temperance, of courage and wisdom, and who said:

> *Why should I fear death? If I am, death is not. If death is, I am not. Why should I fear that which cannot exist when I do?*

I read about Socrates who, when on trial for his life, said, among other things, to his judges these wondrous words:

> *I have not sought during my life to amass wealth and to adorn my body, but I have sought to adorn my soul with the jewels of wisdom, patience, and above all with a love of liberty.*

So, I read about Diogenes, the philosopher who hated the superfluous, the enemy of waste and greed, and who one day entered the temple, reverently approached the altar, crushed a louse between the nails of his thumbs, and solemnly said, "The sacrifice of Diogenes to all the gods." This parodied the worship of the world, satirized all creeds, and, in one act, put the *es-*

sence of religion. Diogenes must have known of this 'inspired' passage: "Without the shedding of blood there is no remission of sins."

I compared Zeno, Epicurus and Socrates—three heathen wretches who had never heard of the Old Testament or the Ten Commandments—with Abraham, Isaac and Jacob—three favorites of Jehovah—and I was depraved enough to think that the Pagans were superior to the Patriarchs, and to Jehovah himself.

VII

My attention was turned to other religions, to the sacred books, the creeds and ceremonies of other lands; of India, Egypt, Assyria, Persia; of the dead and dying nations. I concluded that all religions had the same foundation: a belief in the supernatural, a power above Nature that man could influence by worship, by sacrifice and prayer. I found that all religions rested on a mistaken conception of Nature: that the religion of a people was the science of that people, that is to say, their explanation of the world, of life and death, of origin and destiny.

I concluded that all religions had substantially the same origin, and that in fact there has never been but one religion in the world. The twigs and leaves may differ, but the trunk is the same. The poor African that pours out his heart to a deity of stone is on an exact religious level with the robed priest who supplicates his God. The same mistake, the same superstition, bends the knees and shuts the eyes of both. Both ask for supernatural aid, and neither has the slightest thought of the absolute uniformity of Nature.

It seems probable to me that the first organized ceremonial religion was the worship of the sun. The sun was the 'Sky Father,' the 'All Seeing,' the source of life, the fireside of the world. The sun was regarded as a god who fought the darkness, the power of evil, the enemy of man. There have been many sun-gods, and they seem to have been the chief deities in the ancient religions. They have been worshiped in many lands, by many nations that have passed to death and dust.

Apollo was a sun-god and he fought and conquered the serpent of night. Baldur was a sun-god. He was in love with the Dawn, a maiden. Krishna was a sun-god. At his birth the Ganges was thrilled from its source to the sea, and all the trees, the dead as well as the living, burst into leaf and bud and flower. Hercules was a sun-god and so was Samson, whose strength was in his hair, that is to say, in his beams. He was shorn of his strength by Delilah, the shadow, the darkness. Osiris, Bacchus, and Mithra, Hermes, Buddha, and Quetzalcoatl, Prometheus, Zoroaster, and Perseus,

Cadom, Lao-tzu, Fo-hi, Horus and Rameses, were all sun-gods.

All of these gods had gods for fathers and their mothers were virgins. The births of nearly all were announced by stars, celebrated by celestial music, and voices declared that a blessing had come to the poor world. All of these gods were born in humble places—in caves, under trees, in common inns—and tyrants sought to kill them all when they were babes. All of these sun-gods were born at the winter solstice, on Christmas. Nearly all were worshiped by 'wise men.' All of them fasted for forty days, all of them taught in parables, all of them wrought miracles, all met with a violent death, and all rose from the dead. The history of these gods is the exact history of our Christ. This is not a coincidence, an accident. Christ was a sun-god. Christ was a new name for an old biography—a survival—the last of the sun-gods. Christ was not a man, but a myth; not a life, but a legend.

I found that we had not only borrowed our Christ, but that all our sacraments, symbols and ceremonies were legacies that we received from the buried past. There is nothing original in Christianity.

The cross was a symbol thousands of years before our era. It was a symbol of life, of immortality, of the god Agni; and it was chiseled upon tombs many ages before a line of our Bible was written.

Baptism is far older than Christianity, than Judaism. The Hindus, Egyptians, Greeks and Romans had Holy Water long before a Catholic lived. The eucharist was borrowed from the Pagans. Ceres was the goddess of the fields; Bacchus of the vine. At the harvest festival they made cakes of wheat and said, "This is the flesh of the goddess." They drank wine and cried, "This is the blood of our god."

The Egyptians had a Trinity. They worshiped Osiris, Isis and Horus thousands of years before the Father, Son and Holy Ghost were known. The Tree of Life grew in India, in China, and among the Aztecs, long before the Garden of Eden was planted. Long before our Bible was known, other nations had their sacred books. The dogmas of the Fall of Man, the Atonement and Salvation by Faith, are far older than our religion. In our blessed gospel, in our 'divine scheme,' there is nothing new, nothing original; all old, all borrowed, pieced and patched.

Then I concluded that all religions had been naturally produced, and that all were variation, modifications of one. Then I felt that I knew that all were the work of man.

VIII

The theologians had always insisted that their God was the creator of all living things; that the forms, parts, functions, colors and varieties of animals were the expressions of his fancy, taste and wisdom; that he made them all precisely as they are today; that he invented fins and legs and wings; that he furnished them with the weapons of attack, the shields of defense; that he formed them with reference to food and climate, taking into consideration all facts affecting life.

They insisted that man was a special creation, not related in any way to the animals below him. They also asserted that all the forms of vegetation, from mosses to forests, were just the same today as the moment they were made.

Men of genius, who were for the most part free from religious prejudice, were examining these things, were looking for facts. They were examining the fossils of animals and plants, studying the forms of animals, their bones and muscles, the effect of climate and food, the strange modifications through which they had passed.

Humboldt had published his lectures filled with great thoughts, with splendid generalizations, with suggestions that stimulated the spirit of investigation, and with conclusions that satisfied the mind. He demonstrated the uniformity of Nature, the kinship of all that lives and grows, and that breathes and thinks.

Darwin, with his *Origin of Species*, his theories about Natural Selection, the Survival of the Fittest, and the influence of environment, shed a flood of light upon the great problems of plant and animal life. These things had been guessed, prophesied, asserted, hinted by many others, but Darwin, with infinite patience, with perfect care and candor, found the facts, fulfilled the prophecies, and demonstrated the truth of the guesses, hints and assertions. He was, in my judgment, the keenest observer, the best judge of the meaning and value of a fact, the greatest Naturalist the world has produced. The theological view began to look small and mean.

Spencer gave his theory of evolution and sustained it by countless facts. He stood at a great height, and with the eyes of a philosopher, a profound thinker, surveyed the world. He has influenced the thought of the wisest. Theology looked more absurd than ever.

Huxley entered the lists for Darwin. No man ever had a sharper sword, a better shield. He challenged the world. The great theologians and the small scientists, those who had more courage than sense, accepted the challenge. Their poor bodies were carried away by their friends. Huxley had intelligence, industry, genius, and the courage to express his thought. He was absolutely loyal to what he thought was truth. Without prejudice and without fear, he followed the footsteps of life from the lowest to the highest forms. Theology looked smaller still.

Haeckel began at the simplest cell; went from change to change, from form to form; followed the line of development, the path of life, until he reached the human race. It was all natural. There had been no interference from without.

I read the works of these great men, of many others, and became convinced that they were right, and that all the theologians, all the believers in 'special creation,' were absolutely wrong. The Garden of Eden faded away, Adam and Eve fell back to dust, the snake crawled into the grass, and Jehovah became a miserable myth.

IX

I took another step. What is matter and substance? Can it be destroyed, annihilated? Is it possible to conceive of the destruction of the smallest atom of substance? It can be ground to powder, changed from a solid to a liquid, from a liquid to a gas; but it all remains. Nothing is lost; nothing destroyed. Let an infinite God, if there be one, attack a grain of sand, attack it with infinite power. It cannot be destroyed. It cannot surrender. It defies all force. Substance cannot be destroyed.

Then I took another step. If matter cannot be destroyed, cannot be annihilated, it could not have been created. The indestructible must be uncreateable.

And then I asked myself: What is force? We cannot conceive of the creation of force, or of its destruction. Force may be changed from one form to another, from motion to heat, but it cannot be destroyed, annihilated. If force cannot be destroyed it could not have been created. It is eternal.

Another thing: matter cannot exist apart from force. Force cannot exist apart from matter. Matter could not have existed before force. Force could not have existed before matter. Matter and force can only be conceived of together. This has been shown by several scientists, but most clearly, most forcibly by Buchner. Thought is a form of force; consequently it could not have caused or created matter. Intelligence is a form of force and could not have existed without or apart from matter. Without substance there could have been no mind, no will, no force in any form, and there could have been no substance without force. Matter and force were not created. They have existed from eternity. They cannot be destroyed. There was, there is, no creator.

Then came the question: is there a God? Is there a being of infinite intelligence, power and goodness, who governs the world? There can be goodness without much intelligence, but it seems to me that perfect intelligence and perfect goodness must go together.

In Nature I see, or seem to see, good and evil, intelligence and ignorance, goodness and cruelty, care and carelessness, economy and waste. I see means that do not accomplish the ends, designs that seem to fail. To me it seems infinitely cruel for life to feed on life; to create animals that devour others. The teeth and beaks, the claws and fangs, that tear and rend, fill me with horror. What can be more frightful than a world at war: every leaf a battle-field; every flower a Golgotha; in every drop of water pursuit, capture and death? Under every piece of bark, life lying in wait for life. On every blade of grass something that kills, something that suffers. Everywhere the strong, living on the weak, the superior on the inferior. Everywhere the weak, the insignificant, living on the strong, the inferior on the superior; the highest food for the lowest, man sacrificed for the sake of microbes. Murder universal: everywhere pain, disease and death; death that does not wait for bent forms and gray hairs, but clutches babes and happy youths; death that takes the mother from her helpless, dimpled child; death that fills the world with grief and tears. How can the orthodox Christian explain these things?

I know that life is good. I remember the sunshine and rain. Then I think of the earthquake and flood. I do not forget health and harvest, home and love; but what of pestilence and famine? I cannot harmonize all these contradictions, these blessings and agonies, with the existence of an infinitely good, wise and powerful God.

The theologian says that what we call evil is for our benefit; that we are placed in this world of sin and sorrow to develop character. If this is true I ask why the infant dies? Millions and millions draw a few breaths and fade away in the arms of their mothers. They are not allowed to develop character.

The theologian says that serpents were given fangs to protect themselves from their enemies. Why did the God who made them, make enemies? Why is it that many species of serpents have no fangs?

The theologian says that God armored the hippopotamus, covered his body, except the under part, with scales and plates, so that other animals could not pierce with tooth or tusk. But the same God made the rhinoceros and supplied him with a horn on his nose, with which he disembowels the hippopotamus.

The same God made the eagle, the vulture, the hawk, and their helpless prey. On every hand there seems to be design to defeat design. If God created man—if he is the father of us all—why did he make the criminals, the insane, the deformed and idiotic? Should the inferior man thank God? Should the mother, who clasps to her breast an idiot child, thank God? Should the slave thank God?

The theologian says that God governs the wind, the rain, the lightning. How then can we account for the cyclone, the flood, the drought, the glittering bolt that kills? Suppose we had a man in this country who could control the wind, the rain and lightning, and suppose we elected him to govern these things, and suppose that he allowed whole States to dry and wither, and at the same time wasted the rain in the sea. Suppose that he allowed the winds to destroy cities and to crush to shapelessness thousands of men and women, and allowed the lightnings to strike the life out of mothers and babes. What would we say? What would we think of such a savage? And yet, according to the theologians, this is exactly the course pursued by God. What do we think of a man, who will not, when he has the power, protect his friends? Yet the Christian's God allowed his enemies to torture and burn his friends, his worshipers. Who has ingenuity enough to explain this? What good man, having the power to prevent it, would allow the innocent to be imprisoned, chained in dungeons, and sigh against the dripping walls their weary lives away? If God governs the world, why is innocence not a perfect shield? Why does injustice triumph? Who can answer these questions? In answer, the intelligent, honest man must say: I do not know.

X

This God must be—if he exists—a person, a conscious being. Who can imagine an infinite personality? This God must have force, and we cannot conceive of force apart from matter. This God must be material. He must have the means by which he changes force to what we call thought. When he thinks he uses force, force that must be replaced. Yet we are told that he is infinitely wise. If he is, he does not think. Thought is a ladder, a process by which we reach a conclusion. He who knows all conclusions cannot think. He cannot hope or fear. When knowledge is perfect, there can be no passion, no emotion. If God is infinite he does not want. He has all. He who does not want does not act. The infinite must dwell in eternal calm. It is as impossible to conceive of such a being as to imagine a square triangle, or to think of a circle without a diameter.

Yet we are told that it is our duty to love this God. Can we love the unknown, the inconceivable? Can it be our duty to love anybody? It is our duty to act justly, honestly, but it cannot be our duty to love. We cannot be under obligation to admire a painting, to be charmed with a poem, or thrilled with music. Admiration cannot be controlled. Taste and love are not the servants of the will. Love is, and must be free. It rises from the heart like perfume from a flower. For thousands of ages men and women have been trying to love the gods, trying to soften their hearts, trying to get their aid.

I see them all. The panorama passes before me. I see them with outstretched hands, with reverently closed eyes, worshiping the sun. I see them bowing, in their fear and need, to meteoric stones, imploring serpents, beasts and sacred trees, praying to idols wrought of wood and stone. I see them building altars to the unseen powers, staining them with blood of child and beast. I see the countless priests and hear their solemn chants. I see the dying victims, the smoking altars, the swinging censers, and the rising clouds. I see the half-god men—the mournful Christs—in many lands. I see the common things of life change to miracles as they speed from mouth to mouth. I see the insane prophets reading the secret book of fate by signs and dreams.

I see them all: the Assyrians chanting the praises of Asshur and Ishtar; the Hindus worshiping Brahma, Vishnu and Draupadi; the white-armed—the Chaldeans—sacrificing to Bel and Hea; the Egyptians bowing to Ptah and Fta, Osiris and Isis; the Medes placating the storm, worshiping the fire; the Babylonians supplicating Bel and Murodach. I see them all by the Euphrates, the Tigris, the Ganges and the Nile. I see the Greeks building temples for Zeus, Neptune and Venus. I see the Romans kneeling to a hundred gods. I see others spurning idols and pouring out their hopes and fears to a vague image in the mind.

I see the multitudes, with open mouths, receive as truths the myths and fables of the vanished years. I see them give their toil, their wealth to robe the priests, to build the vaulted roofs, the spacious aisles, the glittering domes. I see them clad in rags, huddled in dens and huts, devouring crusts and scraps, that they may give the more to ghosts and gods.

I see them make their cruel creeds and fill the world with hatred, war, and death. I see them with their faces in the dust in the dark days of plague and sudden death, when cheeks are wan and lips are white for lack of bread.

I hear their prayers, their sighs, and their sobs. I see them kiss the unconscious lips as their hot tears fall on the pallid faces of the dead. I see the nations as they fade and fail. I see them captured and enslaved. I see their altars mingle with the common earth; their temples crumble slowly back to dust. I see their gods grow old and weak, infirm and faint. I see them fall from vague and misty thrones, helpless and dead.

The worshipers receive no help. Injustice triumphs. Toilers are paid with the lash, babes are sold, the innocent stand on scaffolds, and the heroic perish in flames. I see the earthquakes devour, the volcanoes overwhelm, the cyclones wreck, the floods destroy, and the lightnings kill.

The nations perished. The gods died. The toil and wealth were lost. The temples were built in vain, and all the prayers died unanswered in the heedless air.

Then I asked myself the question: Is there a supernatural power, an arbitrary mind, an enthroned God, a supreme will that sways the tides and currents of the world to which all causes bow?

I do not deny. I do not know. But I do not believe. I believe that the natural is supreme; that from the infinite chain no link can be lost or broken; that there is no supernatural power that can answer prayer, no power that worship can persuade or change, no power that cares for man.

I believe that with infinite arms Nature embraces the all; that there is no interference, no chance; that behind every event are the necessary and countless causes; and that beyond every event will be and must be the necessary and countless effects.

Man must protect himself. He cannot depend upon the supernatural, upon an imaginary father in the skies. He must protect himself by finding the facts in Nature, by developing his brain, to the end that he may overcome the obstructions and take advantage of the forces of Nature.

Is there a God? I do not know. Is man immortal? I do not know. One thing I do know, and that is that neither hope nor fear, belief nor denial can change the fact. It is as it is, and it will be as it must be. We wait and hope.

XI

When I became convinced that the Universe is natural, that all the ghosts and gods are myths, there entered into my brain—into my soul, into every drop of my blood—the sense, the feeling, the joy of freedom. The walls of my prison crumbled and fell, the dungeon was flooded with light and all the bolts, and bars, and manacles became dust. I was no longer a servant, a serf or a slave. There was for me no master in all the wide world, not even in infinite space. I was free—free to think, to express my thoughts; free to live to my own ideal; free to live for myself and those I loved; free to use all my faculties, all my senses; free to spread imagination's wings; free to investigate, to guess and dream and hope; free to judge and determine for myself; free to reject all ignorant and cruel creeds, all the 'inspired' books that savages have produced, and all the barbarous legends of the past; free from popes and priests; free from all the 'called' and 'set apart;' free from sanctified mistakes and holy lies; free from the fear of eternal pain; free from

the winged monsters of the night; free from devils, ghosts and gods.

For the first time I was free. There were no
prohibited places in all the realms of thought;
no air, no space, where fancy could not spread
her painted wings; no chains for my limbs; no
lashes for my back; no fires for my flesh; no
master's frown or threat; no following another's steps; no need to bow, or cringe, or crawl,
or utter lying words. I was free. I stood erect
fearlessly, joyously, and faced all worlds.

And then my heart was filled with gratitude,
with thankfulness, and went out in love to all
the heroes, the thinkers who gave their lives for
the liberty of hand and brain; for the freedom
of labor and thought; to those who fell on the
fierce fields of war, to those who died in dungeons bound with chains; to those who proudly
mounted scaffold stairs; to those whose bones
were crushed, whose flesh was scarred and torn;
to those by fire consumed; to all the wise, the
good, the brave of every land, whose thoughts
and deeds have given freedom to the sons of
men. And then I vowed to grasp the torch that
they had held, and hold it high, that light might
conquer darkness still.

Let us be true to ourselves, true to the facts we know; and let us, above all things, preserve the veracity of our souls. If there be gods, we cannot help them, but we can assist our fellow-men. We cannot love the inconceivable, but we can love wife and child and friend. We can be as honest as we are ignorant. If we are, when asked what is beyond the horizon of the known, we must say that we do not know. We can tell the truth, and we can enjoy the blessed freedom that the brave have won. We can destroy the monsters of superstition, the hissing snakes of ignorance and fear. We can drive from our minds the frightful things that tear and wound with beak and fang. We can civilize our fellow-men. We can fill our lives with generous deeds, with loving words, with art and song, and all the ecstasies of love. We can flood our years with sunshine, with the divine climate of kindness, and we can drain to the last drop the golden cup of joy.

Preface to the Dresden Edition
Robert Green Ingersoll

The following is from the Preface to *The Works of Robert G. Ingersoll*, a twelve-volume edition (the Dresden Edition) published by Farrell, New York.

These lectures have been so maimed and mutilated by orthodox malice; have been made to appear so halt, crotchety and decrepit by those who mistake the pleasures of calumny for the duties of religion, that in simple justice to myself I have concluded to publish them.

Most of the clergy are, or seem to be, utterly incapable of discussing anything in a fair and catholic spirit. They appeal, not to reason, but to prejudice; not to facts, but to passages of scripture. They can conceive of no goodness, of no spiritual exaltation beyond the horizon of their creed. Whoever differs with them upon what they are pleased to call 'fundamental truths,' is, in their opinion, a base and infamous man. To re-enact the tragedies of the sixteenth century, they lack only the power. Bigotry in all ages has been the same. Christianity simply transferred the brutality of the Colosseum to the Inquisition. For the murderous combat of the gladiators, the saints substituted the *auto de fe*. What has been called religion is, after all, but the organization of the wild beast in man. The perfumed blossom of arrogance is heaven. Hell is the consummation of revenge.

The chief business of the clergy has always been to destroy the joy of life, and multiply and magnify the terrors and tortures of death and perdition. They have polluted the heart and paralyzed the brain; and upon the ignorant altars of the Past and the Dead, they have endeavored to sacrifice the Present and the Living.

Nothing can exceed the mendacity of the religious press. I have had some little experience with political editors, and am forced to say, that until I read the religious papers, I did not know what malicious and slimy falsehoods could be constructed from ordinary words. The ingenuity with which the real and apparent meaning can be tortured out of language, is simply amazing. The average religious editor is intolerant and insolent; he knows nothing of affairs; he has the envy of failure, the malice of impotence, and always accounts for the brave and generous actions of unbelievers by low, base and unworthy motives.

By this time, even the clergy should know that the intellect of the nineteenth century needs no guardian. They should cease to regard themselves as shepherds defending flocks of weak, silly and fearful sheep from the claws and teeth of ravening wolves. By this time, they should know that the religion of the ignorant and brutal past no longer satisfies the heart and brain; that the miracles have become contemptible; that the 'evidences' have ceased to convince; that the spirit of investigation cannot be stopped nor stayed; that the church is losing her power; that the young are holding in a kind of tender contempt the sacred follies of the old; that the pulpit and pews no longer represent the culture and morality of the world, and that the brand of intellectual inferiority is upon the orthodox brain.

Men should be liberated from the aristocracy of the air. Every chain of superstition should be broken. The rights of men and women should be equal and sacred; marriage should be a perfect partnership; children should be governed by kindness; every family should be a republic; every fireside a democracy.

It seems almost impossible for religious people to really grasp the idea of intellectual freedom. They seem to think that man is responsible for his honest thoughts; that unbelief is a crime; that investigation is sinful; that credulity is a virtue, and that reason is a dangerous guide. They cannot divest themselves of the idea that in the realm of thought there must be government—authority and obedience; laws and penalties; rewards and punishments—and that somewhere in the universe there is a penitentiary for the soul.

In the republic of the mind, one is a majority. There, all are monarchs and all are equals. The tyranny of a majority even is unknown. Each one is crowned, sceptered and throned. Upon every brow is the tiara, and around every form is the imperial purple. Only those are good citizens who express their honest thoughts, and those who persecute for opinion's sake are the only traitors. There, nothing is considered infamous except an appeal to brute force, and nothing sacred but love, liberty, and joy.

The church contemplates this republic with a sneer. From the teeth of hatred she draws back the lips of scorn. She is filled with the spite and spleen born of intellectual weakness. Once she was egotistic; now she is envious. Once she wore upon her hollow breast false gems, supposing them to be real. They have been shown to be false, but she wears them still. She has the malice of the caught, the hatred of the exposed.

We are told to investigate the Bible for ourselves, and at the same time informed that if we come to the conclusion that it is not the inspired word of God, we will most assuredly be damned. Under such circumstances, if we believe this, investigation is impossible. Whoever is held responsible for his conclusions cannot weigh the evidence with impartial scales. Fear stands at the balance, and gives to falsehood the weight of its trembling hand.

I oppose the church because she is the enemy of liberty; because her dogmas are infamous and cruel; because she humiliates and degrades woman; because she teaches the doctrines of eternal torment and the natural depravity of man; because she insists upon the absurd, the impossible, and the senseless; because she resorts to falsehood and slander; because she is arrogant and revengeful; because she allows men to sin on a credit; because she discourages self-reliance, and laughs at good works; because she believes in vicarious virtue and vicarious vice—vicarious punishment and vicarious reward; because she regards repentance of more importance than restitution; and because she sacrifices the world we have to one we know not of.

The free and generous, the tender and affectionate, will understand me. Those who have escaped from the grated cells of a creed will appreciate my motives. The sad and suffering wives, the trembling and loving children will thank me. This is enough.

Afterword

Robert Green Ingersoll (1833-1899) was a prodigious intellectual figure of the late nineteenth century. His output—the writings and orations—was equally prodigious. Ingersoll was a man not unlike the earlier giant, Thomas Paine, an unceasing thinker, part philosopher and part rebel, but fully dedicated to freedom and truth.

This small volume, contemporaneously re-titled *God: Hit or Myth?*, is adapted from a famous Ingersoll oration first delivered in 1896. It has been modified only as necessary to satisfy the adaptation from the structure, format and punctuation of the speech to the essay. No substantive deletions or additions have been made in the editing process.

Of particular interest is the striking contemporaneity of Robert Green Ingersoll's observations and arguments with the debates and ideological struggles occurring in the United States and, indeed, worldwide in the first decades of the twenty-first century. His reasoning is as cogent now as it was then.

Yet, Ingersoll's reasoning is not a definitive answer to the question of the non-existence of God and gods. That question is, perhaps, the most complex of all the philosophic constructs created by the human mind and one that will inflame humankind forever without resolution. But Ingersoll does offer an opening, a place to begin, in the process of reasoned investigation and the rational evaluation of belief.

Robert Green Ingersoll titled this 1896 oration and the subsequent essay, *Why I Am an Agnostic*. The original oration was separate from a two-part essay he wrote titled *Why Am I an Agnostic?* The two perspectives—one a question and one a statement—to the central question of belief give an indication of Ingersoll's strengthening affirmation in the mythology of gods and religions, and the truth of Nature's dominance over mankind.

It is important that Ingersoll's position be understood. He was an agnostic, that is, one who holds that any ultimate reality (as God or gods) is unknown and probably unknowable. The term *agnostic* was first introduced by Huxley in 1869, although Ingersoll is often referred to as "The Father of Agnosticism."

It is not clear whether Ingersoll was an atheist, that is, one who denies the existence of God or gods. If one proceeds from the atheistic position of a disbelief in the existence of a deity, it is not an excessive leap from agnosticism to atheism, especially proceeding from the impassioned writings of Robert Green Ingersoll. The term *atheist* predates *agnostic* by almost three hundred years, having first been used in 1571.

The myriad philosophic constructs surrounding atheism and agnosticism will never be absolute; the debate will continue forever. Humankind is incapable of either understanding the constructs or agreeing on any belief or disbelief system. Whether the most recent attempt at understanding belief is called Darwinism or Intelligent Design, Christianity or Islam, or any other label for the religious partitioning and control of the human mind, the logic continues to weigh heavily in the balance of reason, favoring Nature as the only universal force.

Ian Tarquin Hume
Inverness, Scotland
April 16, 2006

Robert Green Ingersoll

Ingersoll, Robert Green, 1833–99, American orator and lawyer, b. Dresden, N.Y. The son of a Congregational minister who settled eventually in Illinois, Ingersoll was admitted (1854) to the bar and became a court lawyer. He served in the Union army during the Civil War. Although previously a Democrat, he emerged from the war a Republican, and in 1876 he nominated James G. Blaine for President in his famous 'Plumed Knight' speech. He served (1867–69) as attorney general of Illinois, but his antireligious beliefs prevented any further advance. Known as 'the great agnostic,' Ingersoll questioned the tenets of Christian belief in such lectures as "The Gods" (1872), "Some Mistakes of Moses" (1879), "Why I Am an Agnostic" (1896), and "Superstition" (1898), drawing large audiences through his eloquence and provoking denunciations from the orthodox. One of the greatest orators of his day, Ingersoll was acclaimed by Henry Ward Beecher as the "most brilliant speaker of the English tongue of all the men on the globe." His lectures were widely read for a generation, and editions of his works still circulate; the Dresden edition (twelve vol., 1900) has been reprinted several times.

Encyclopedia information about Robert G. Ingersoll, *The Columbia Electronic Encyclopedia*, Sixth Edition Copyright © 2003, Columbia University Press.

Notes

Notes

The text of this book is composed in 10-point ITC New Baskerville, a modern interpretation of the original types cut in 1762 by British type founder and printer John Baskerville. During the centuries since its creation, Baskerville has remained one of the world's most widely used typefaces.

The paper used is 60# Nature's Natural, a fifty percent post-consumer recycled paper, processed chlorine-free.

The book's printer, Thomson-Shore, Inc., is a member of Green Press Initiative, a nonprofit program dedicated to supporting authors, publishers, and suppliers in their efforts to reduce the use of paper fiber obtained from endangered forests.